RILEY'S
BOOK SWAP
CORONA
BEACH

Visual Geography Series®

NEPAL

...in Pictures

Prepared by
Geography Department

Lerner Publications Company
Minneapolis

Copyright © 1989 by Lerner Publications Company

All rights reserved. International copyright secured. No part of this book may be reproduced, stored in a retrieval system, or transmitted in any form or by any means—electronic, mechanical, photocopying, recording, or otherwise—without the prior written permission of the publisher, except for the inclusion of brief quotations in an acknowledged review.

Photo by Bernice K. Condit

Shoppers stroll through a market in Kathmandu, the capital of Nepal.

This is an all-new edition of the Visual Geography Series. Previous editions have been published by Sterling Publishing Company, New York City, and some of the original textual information has been retained. New photographs, maps, charts, captions, and updated information have been added. The text has been entirely reset in 10/12 Century Textbook.

LIBRARY OF CONGRESS CATALOGING-IN-PUBLICATION DATA

Nepal in pictures.
        (Visual geography series)
        Rev. ed. of: Nepal, Sikkim, and Bhutan (Himalayan kingdoms) in pictures / Eugene Gordon.
        Includes Index.
        Summary: Discusses the land, history, government, people, and economy of the country whose diverse topography contains the world's highest peak and also lush tropical lowlands.
        1. Nepal. [1. Nepal] I. Gordon, Eugene, 1923– Nepal, Sikkim, and Bhutan (Himalayan kingdoms) in pictures. II. Lerner Publications Company. Geography Dept. III. Series: Visual geography series (Minneapolis, Minn.)
DS493.4.N482 1989   954.9'6   88-8347
ISBN 0-8225-1851-1

International Standard Book Number: 0-8225-1851-1
Library of Congress Catalog Card Number: 88-8347

VISUAL GEOGRAPHY SERIES®

Publisher
Harry Jonas Lerner
Associate Publisher
Nancy M. Campbell
Senior Editor
Mary M. Rodgers
Editor
Gretchen Bratvold
Assistant Editors
Dan Filbin
Kathleen S. Heidel
Photo Researcher
Karen A. Sirvaitis
Editorial/Photo Assistant
Marybeth Campbell
Consultants/Contributors
J. David Smith
Sandra K. Davis
Designer
Jim Simondet
Cartographer
Carol F. Barrett
Indexer
Kristine S. Schubert
Production Manager
Richard J. Hannah

Courtesy of Heidi Larson/UNICEF

Two children from the Kathmandu Valley play dice on a game board of painted burlap.

Acknowledgments

Title page photo courtesy of Todd T. Lewis.

Elevation contours adapted from *The Times Atlas of the World*, seventh comprehensive edition (New York: Times Books, 1985).

1 2 3 4 5 6 7 8 9 10 98 97 96 95 94 93 92 91 90 89

Photo by Daniel H. Condit

Pashupatinath—the largest and holiest Hindu shrine in Nepal—is located three miles east of Kathmandu on the sacred Bagmati River. Pashupati, or lord of the animals, represents Siva, the Hindu god of creation and destruction.

Contents

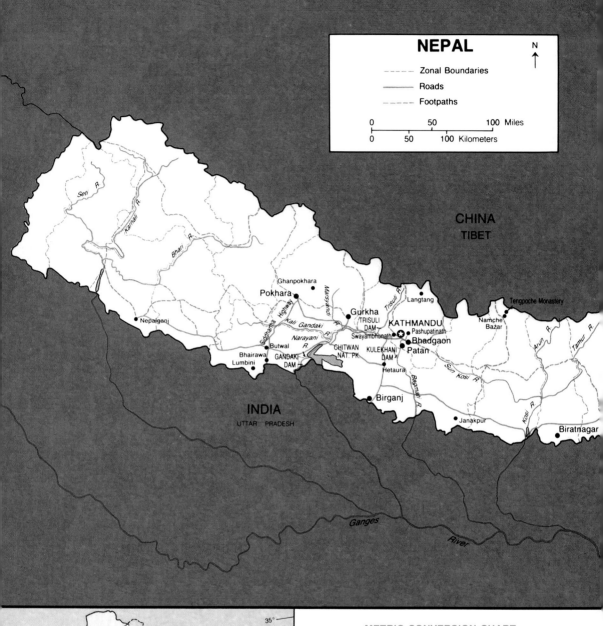

NEPAL

N

- – – – Zonal Boundaries
- ——— Roads
- – – – Footpaths

| 0 | 50 | 100 Miles |
| 0 | 50 | 100 Kilometers |

CHINA
TIBET

Seti R.

Karnali R.

Bhari R.

Ghanpokhara
Pokhara
Nepalganj
Marsyandi R.
Gurkha
TRISULI DAM
Langtang
Trisuli R.
Tengpoche Monastery
Namche Bazar
KATHMANDU
Swayambhunath Pashupatinath
Bhadgaon
Patan
Siddhartha Highway
Kali Gandaki R.
Butwal
Narayani R.
CHITWAN NAT. PK.
KULEKHANI DAM
GANDAKI DAM
Bhairawa
Lumbini
Hetaura
Arun R.
Tamur R.
Sun Kosi R.
Baghmati R.
Kosi R.
Birganj

INDIA
UTTAR PRADESH
Janakpur
Biratnagar

Ganges River

35°
30°
25°
20°
15°
10°
5°

BAY OF BENGAL

SOUTH ASIA
NEPAL

INDIAN OCEAN

65° 70° 75° 80° 85° 90° 95°

| 0 | 500 Miles |
| 0 | 500 Kilometers |

METRIC CONVERSION CHART
To Find Approximate Equivalents

WHEN YOU KNOW:	MULTIPLY BY:	TO FIND:
AREA		
acres	0.41	hectares
square miles	2.59	square kilometers
CAPACITY		
gallons	3.79	liters
LENGTH		
feet	30.48	centimeters
yards	0.91	meters
miles	1.61	kilometers
MASS (weight)		
pounds	0.45	kilograms
tons	0.91	metric tons
VOLUME		
cubic yards	0.77	cubic meters
TEMPERATURE		
degrees Fahrenheit	0.56 (*after* subtracting 32)	degrees Celsius

Photo by Josh Kohnstamm

A Nepalese woman kneels before a statue of Buddha, which means "Enlightened One." Buddhism, founded in India by Gautama Buddha in the sixth century B.C., strongly influences the spiritual lives of the Nepalese and coexists with Hinduism, one of the world's oldest belief systems.

Introduction

With a history spanning more than 2,000 years, Nepal is a land of extreme contrasts in south central Asia. A Hindu kingdom, Nepal was a forbidden realm from 1846 until 1951. Only a handful of outsiders were permitted to enter the country during the 100-year rule of the Ranas—hereditary prime ministers who had seized the king's power. This period of isolation from outside contact spared Nepal from colonization by European powers. It also seriously hindered the country's economic and social development—a consequence from which Nepal is still recovering.

By 1951 an anti-Rana movement had placed the king back in power and had ended Nepal's long isolation. Tourists, at-tracted by the rugged beauty of the Himalaya Mountains—which contain the world's highest peaks—soon began to enter the country. They found a beautiful land whose people had a rich mix of cultural, ethnic, and religious characteristics. Through tourism and other foreign contact, the Nepalese learned of technological advances in the rest of the world.

Many influences have shaped the lifestyles of the ethnic groups in present-day Nepal. From the south and west came Indians, who followed the Hindu religion. Tibetans, who practiced their own local beliefs, entered the region from the north and east. After the sixth century B.C., Buddhism, a religious philosophy founded

Photo by David Tykol

by Gautama Buddha, arrived from India. Later the Nepalese would convert their Tibetan neighbors to Buddhism.

Throughout much of Nepal's history, small local kingdoms were very tolerant of these diverse influences. As a result, many ethnic groups arose in the region, and each formed a unique society that molded aspects of the Indian and Tibetan cultures to its own lifestyle.

Although political parties do not exist in Nepal, elected councils called panchayats have helped to unify the nation's peoples by giving them a democratic voice. Some Nepalese criticize the panchayat system, citing the nation's inability to solve economic and social problems as evidence of the government's ineffectiveness. Yet no government would be able to quickly solve the pressing problems of Nepal—one of the poorest countries in the world.

In Bhadgaon—one of Nepal's oldest towns—a costumed dancer wears an elaborate mask and headdress.

Members of a village council, or panchayat, meet with a forestry agent to discuss the planting of quickly maturing trees. Indiscriminate woodcutting has created serious soil erosion in Nepal.

Courtesy of F. Botts/FAO

Courtesy of Nepal Department of Tourism, Kathmandu

Pleats of snow blanket the uppermost reaches of a peak in the Himalayas—the tallest mountains on earth. The name *Himalaya* comes from the Sanskrit language of India and means "abode of snow."

1) The Land

Nepal is a landlocked country in southern Asia nestled among the Himalayas, the highest mountain chain in the world. The country is approximately 500 miles long and 100 miles wide. Covering an area of 54,362 square miles, Nepal is slightly smaller than the state of Florida. Tibet—a province that is called Xizang by the Chinese, who annexed the region in 1959—borders Nepal to the north. India forms Nepal's eastern, southern, and western boundaries.

Topography

Extreme contrasts characterize the topography of Nepal. Within just 100 miles, al-titudes range from 200 feet above sea level in the south to 29,028 feet on top of Mount Everest—the highest point on the earth. This dramatic peak emerged millions of years ago when the Indian subcontinent collided into the stationary Asian conti-nent. Although the Himalaya Mountains arose primarily from 2 to 65 million years ago, earthquakes occur frequently in the region, and the mountains continue to rise up. Nepal contains three topographic re-gions from south to north—the terai, the hills, and the mountains.

TERAI

With a tropical climate and lush vegeta-tion, the lowland strip known as the terai

7

runs along Nepal's southern border. An extension of the Ganges Plain of northern India, much of the region consists of flat, fertile land that provides most of the nation's food. Elevations in the terai vary from 200 to 600 feet above sea level. Numerous streams that begin in the mountains cross the region. The waterways carry tons of silt, sand, gravel, and boulders to the plain.

After health programs in the 1950s and 1960s reduced the threat of malaria, many Nepalese farmers migrated to the fertile terai. The increased population has placed a burden on the land. Many of the forests that once covered the region have been cleared for farming and for firewood. As a result, the forests are quickly disappearing, and the loss of topsoil through erosion is decreasing the quality of the land.

HILLS

The terai is only 55 miles across at its widest point, and along its northern edge the Siwalik Range rises to nearly 5,000 feet above sea level. Part of the Outer Himalayas, this upland area begins Nepal's hill region. To the north, the Mahabharat Range ascends to heights of 10,000 feet. Swiftly flowing mountain rivers have carved deep valleys throughout the hills.

Near the center of the hill region lies the Kathmandu Valley—a circular basin that once contained a lake. Covering 218 square miles, this valley is the largest flat area outside of the terai and is another important agricultural region. The Himalayas protect the valley from icy winter winds from the north, and the Mahabharat Range shields it from the summer monsoon (a

Photo by Bernice K. Condit

Houses line an unpaved road in Butwal, a town in the terai, Nepal's southernmost region. Situated along the north central border of the terai, Butwal has a hilly terrain characteristic of the outermost edges of the vast Himalaya Mountains.

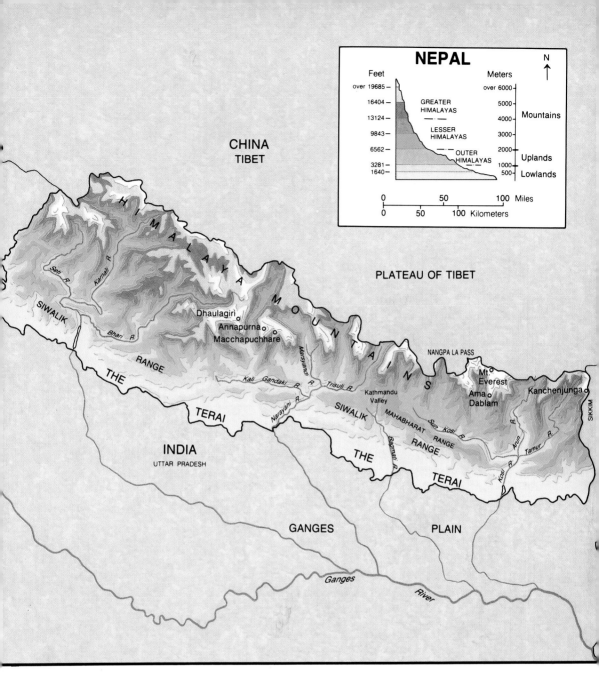

NEPAL

N

Feet		Meters
over 19685 —		over 6000—
16404 —	GREATER HIMALAYAS	5000— Mountains
13124 —	LESSER HIMALAYAS	4000—
9843 —		3000—
6562 —	OUTER HIMALAYAS	2000— Uplands
3281 —		1000—
1640 —		500— Lowlands

0   50   100 Miles
0   50   100 Kilometers

CHINA
TIBET

PLATEAU OF TIBET

HIMALAYA MOUNTAINS

Sefi R.
Karnali R.
SIWALIK
Bheri R.
RANGE
THE
TERAI
INDIA
UTTAR PRADESH

Dhaulagiri
Annapurna
Macchapuchhare
Marsyandi
Kali Gandaki R.
Trisuli R.
Narayani R.
SIWALIK
Kathmandu Valley
MAHABHARAT RANGE
Bagmati R.
THE
TERAI
PLAIN

NANGPA LA PASS
Mt. Everest
Ama Dablam
Kanchenjunga
Sun Kosi R.
Arun R.
Tamur R.
Kosi R.
SIKKIM

GANGES

Ganges River

---

strong, seasonal wind that carries rain) from the south.

MOUNTAINS

The highest regions in Nepal are part of the Greater Himalayas, which average 20,000 feet above sea level. Between this chain and the Outer Himalayas to the south, the Lesser Himalayas range from 6,500 to 13,000 feet in elevation. The entire mountain system extends in a 1,500-mile arc from northeastern Pakistan to northeastern India, and, in some sections, it spans 200 miles in width.

The Nepalese Himalayas contain Mount Everest (known as Sagamartha in Nepal), which at 29,028 feet is the world's highest peak. Several other summits within Nepal or along its borders—including Kanchenjunga (28,146 feet), Dhaulagiri (26,810 feet), and Annapurna (26,504 feet)—are among the world's highest peaks.

Rivers

A network of streams and rivers crisscrosses Nepal, draining the melting snows of the Himalayas and the heavy rains of the hills. Eventually, these waterways empty into the Ganges River in northern India. Three separate river systems—the Kosi, the Narayani, and the Karnali—begin on the Plateau of Tibet. The Kosi waters eastern Nepal and has seven major tributaries, the longest of which are the Arun, the Sun Kosi, and the Tamur. During the rainy season from June to September, the Kosi overflows its banks as it moves across the terai, leaving heavy deposits of silt behind.

The Narayani cuts through central Nepal, and some of its tributaries—such as the Kali Gandaki, Trisuli, and Marsyandi—carve some of the deepest gorges in the world. At high altitudes, shallow basins connected by waterfalls provide ideal conditions for the generation of hydroelectric power. Small steamships and timber barges navigate the lower Narayani when it is not flooded.

The Karnali River in western Nepal is also noted for its deep gorges. The waterway and its tributaries—including the Bhari and Seti—isolate rather than connect settlements along their paths because the river canyons are too wide for suspension bridges. Furthermore, the currents are too rapid for safe navigation by canoe.

Climate

The southwest monsoon affects Nepal's weather. This strong wind carries heavy rainfall northwest from the Bay of Bengal from June to September. As the moist air carried by the monsoon rises, it condenses and falls as rain. Because the monsoon deposits much of its moisture before it reaches high elevations, Nepal is dry in the mountains and in western areas of the country. Middle and low elevations, however, receive adequate rainfall.

Courtesy of United Nations

Porters (load carriers) carefully make their way across a rushing river on a makeshift bridge. Heavy monsoon rains flood many rivers in the summer, making travel impossible in some places.

Nepal's greatly varied topography also affects the weather, producing a wide range of conditions. Elevation influences the temperature as well as the amount of rainfall. Temperatures generally drop as altitude increases. Exposure to sunlight and to moisture-laden monsoon winds—which is greater on the eastern sides of the mountain ridges—further influences weather patterns.

The terai experiences hot, humid weather during the monsoon season from June to September. The region receives 80 percent of its annual rainfall during the monsoon. Temperatures during this period average 80° F in the eastern portion of the country and 90° F in the drier western section. From October through February temperatures are moderately cool with scattered showers. A dry season occurs in the terai from March to June.

In the hills, at elevations of about 4,000 to 10,000 feet, summers are warm and rainy and winters are chilly and dry. The Kathmandu Valley has a rainy season from June to September, a cold season from October to April, and a hot season in May and June. In January, the coldest month, temperatures range between 36° and 64° F, and they occasionally reach a high of 90° F in May and June.

Himalayan regions above 10,000 feet endure long, severe winters. In some areas the frost never thaws, and summers are short and cool, with an average temperature of 45° F. The snow line, beyond which snow covers the ground year-round, begins between 12,000 and 16,000 feet, depending on the amount of moisture an area receives.

Flora and Fauna

Like the climate, the distribution of flora and fauna in Nepal depends on altitude and moisture levels. Elephants, rhinoceroses, leopards, tigers, deer, crocodiles, and many kinds of snakes inhabit the forests and swamps of the tropical terai. Stands

Photo by David Tykol

This Asian rhinoceros, with its characteristic armorlike folds of skin, lives in Nepal's Chitwan National Park.

of hardwood and bamboo thrive in areas that have not been cleared for agriculture. Sal trees, whose wood resembles teak, are among several kinds of commercially valuable timber in the region.

Above 4,000 feet, the gradual decrease in temperature has a corresponding effect on vegetation and wildlife. The tropical forest changes to a temperate zone, where pine and oak trees thrive and where wild boar, wildcats, foxes, and a wide variety of birds live. Between elevations of 5,000 and 10,000 feet, walnuts, chestnuts, maples, wild cherries, firs, birches, rhododendrons, larches, and some bamboos grow.

At about 12,000 to 13,000 feet above sea level the trees disappear. Only grasses, moss lichens, and tiny alpine flowers can survive in the cold, dry regions above the tree line. But animals—including foxes, wild goats, snow partridges, snow cocks, and snow leopards—are still abundant.

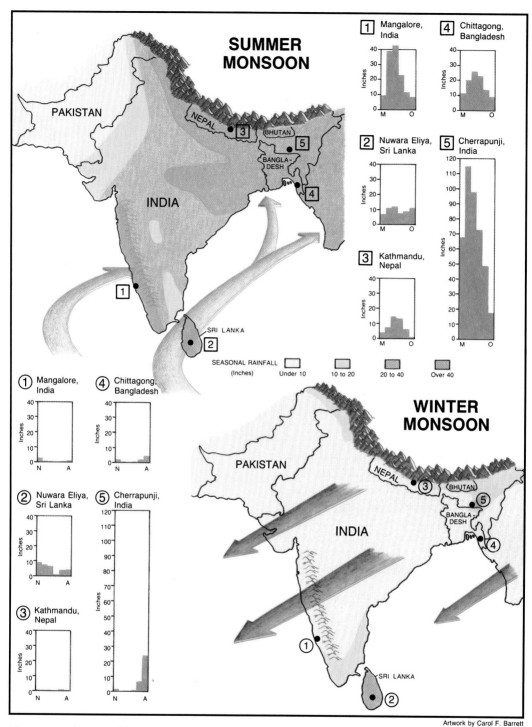

Artwork by Carol F. Barrett

These maps show the shift of seasonal winds—called monsoons—over southern Asia and the rainfall levels for five cities in the region. In summer (May to October), the monsoon blows from sea to land, carrying moisture that is released as rain as it passes over this part of the Asian continent. In winter (November to April), the monsoon blows from land to sea. Because they originate over a cold, arid land surface, the winter winds are dry, and little or no rainfall is associated with them. Kathmandu, Nepal, has the classic monsoon rainfall pattern. Large amounts of rain occur in the summer months, when the moisture-bearing winds blow from the south, and small amounts of rain fall in the winter months, when dry winds come from the north. Kathmandu's summer is not quite as wet as the southeastern terai's because by the time the winds reach Kathmandu they have already lost some of their moisture. Climate data taken from *World-Climates* by Willy Rudloff, Stuttgart, 1981.

Photo by David Tykol

Poinsettias flourish in the Himalayan foothills.

Beyond the tree line, up to 16,000 feet, the most important animal is the yak, a relative of the cow and the buffalo. Yaks measure up to six feet high at the shoulder, weigh about 1,000 pounds, and have short legs, long shaggy hair, and curved horns.

The wide variety of birds found in Nepal is partly due to the country's many different altitude and rainfall zones. Nepal's location along migratory routes for birds from southern and northern Asia also attracts an abundance of winged species.

Cities

The Kathmandu Valley, home to a large percentage of Nepal's population, contains most of the nation's urban areas. The cities of Kathmandu, Patan, and Bhadgaon have each served as the capital during the long line of kingdoms in the valley's history. All three cities remain the major communities in the valley, with Kathmandu serving as the modern capital.

Photo by David Tykol

A vulture soars over central Nepal near the town of Ghanpokhara.

13

With 93 percent of Nepal's population living in rural communities, numerous settlements are scattered throughout the country. The only large town outside of the Kathmandu Valley is Biratnagar, an industrial and commercial center in the eastern terai with 90,000 inhabitants. Janakpur, Birganj, and Nepalganj serve as regional market centers in the terai.

KATHMANDU

Legend says that King Gunakamadeva founded Kathmandu, the capital of Nepal, in the eighth century A.D. Until the sixteenth century the city was known as Kantipur (City of Glory). Its modern name derives from Kastmandap, a temple near Durbar Square in the heart of the city. Located at about 4,500 feet above sea level, Kathmandu has temperate weather most of the year. Its population of over 420,000 people makes it the largest metropolitan area in Nepal.

Kathmandu has many new buildings and hotels, but the old section of the city still flourishes. Its narrow alleyways and streets are crowded with shops and streetsellers. Durbar Square, which stood at the center of Kathmandu in ancient times, remains the focal point of the old section of the city. Scattered around this square are some of the capital's finest temples, palaces, and old public buildings.

A short distance from Kathmandu, on the road to the town of Bodnath, is Pashupatinath—the holiest temple for Nepalese Hindus. Situated on the banks of the Bagmati River—considered a sacred waterway by Nepalese Hindus—Pashupatinath attracts pilgrims from all over the country.

Photo by David Tykol

People crowd a street in the old section of Kathmandu, which displays many examples of centuries-old architecture and wood carving.

Photo by Bernice K. Condit

Worshippers in Patan enter and leave a Hindu temple by way of an elaborate courtyard.

Photo by Ruthi Soudack

As the family of the deceased looks on, a priest sets a funeral pyre ablaze on a ghat (platform) along the Bagmati River. Hindus believe that cremation helps free the soul from the body. Afterward, the ashes are sprinkled on the sacred waters of the river.

Photo by David Tykol

From a village in Nepal's central hill region, snow-covered peaks of the distant Himalayas rise against northern skies. Ninety-three percent of the Nepalese people live in rural areas.

They come to worship Pashupati, lord of the animals and representative of Siva, the Hindu god of destruction and rebirth. Dying Hindus frequently come to the area to spend their last days. Funeral ghats (plat-forms) line the banks of the river. Hindus burn their dead on these ghats and then sprinkle the ashes in the water. The Nepalese also use the Bagmati River daily for bathing and for washing clothes.

PATAN

With a population of about 100,000, Patan (known as Lalitpur in the Sanskrit language) is located three miles south of Kathmandu. Once an independent kingdom, Patan's history spans 2,000 years. The city spreads out from its royal palace, and four main roads lead from this center to the four corners of Patan. Stupas—Buddhist shrines said to have been built by the Indian emperor Asoka in the third century B.C.—mark the northern, eastern, southern, and western limits of the city.

The home of Newar craftspeople, Patan remains a Buddhist city and the major artistic center of Nepal. Elaborate pagodas (temples), decorative wood carvings, and ornate religious shrines line the narrow, winding streets of Patan. More than one-third of its inhabitants are farmers, and many others engage in craft industries, which they operate from their homes. Some residents of Patan commute to work in Kathmandu each day.

BHADGAON

Bhadgaon (called Bhaktapur in Sanskrit) is nine miles east of Kathmandu. Founded in the ninth century by King Anandamalla along an ancient trade route to Tibet, Bhadgaon served as the capital of the Kathmandu Valley from the fourteenth to the sixteenth centuries. The city has historically been more isolated from outside influences than have Kathmandu and Patan. As a result, Bhadgaon has preserved its age-old character even better than the other two urban centers have.

Bhadgaon's 60,000 people are also more self-sufficient than are those of other valley communities. Local farmers grow the city's food, local craftspeople construct and decorate its buildings, and local traders fulfill its commercial needs. A showcase of ancient art and architecture, Bhadgaon boasts sculpture and wood carving, as well as colossal pagodas in which the Nepalese worship various gods and goddesses.

Photo by Bernice K. Condit

Residents of Bhadgaon are able to meet the needs of their community, which buys little from other areas of the country. Here, women thresh a recently harvested crop of rice, the mainstay of the Nepalese diet.

The stupa (Buddhist shrine) of Swayambhunath rises at the top of a small hill west of Kathmandu—a site that has been considered sacred for more than 2,500 years. On all four sides of the structure the painted eyes of Buddha gaze across the valley, signifying his presence everywhere. Between the heavy black brows is a third eye that symbolizes true wisdom. The nose is the Nepalese number *ek,* meaning "one"—a symbol of unity. Buddhism has influenced Nepalese life for 2,000 years.

Photo by David Tykol

2) History and Government

Nearly all of the known early historical events in Nepal happened in the Kathmandu Valley. Many gaps exist in the nation's early history because the people living in the region did not keep accurate records until the eighteenth century. No written sources of any kind exist before the fifth century A.D. Although oral legends and folktales capture the flavor of life in the region prior to the fifth century, historians cannot prove that these accounts reflect actual events.

In the sixteenth century the Nepalese collected these stories into written chronicles, or *vamsavalis,* which comprise the most complete account of Nepalese history. Foreign writers from India and China have confirmed some of the events in the vamsavalis through their own historical records. Indeed, Indian and Chinese rulers had authority over Nepal during some periods of its history.

The Kiratis

Living primarily as nomadic herders and farmers, Nepal's earliest immigrants probably were the Kiratis, who came from northeastern India in the seventh or eighth century B.C. The Kiratis cleared the land for agriculture by cutting and burning vegetation. They moved on every few years to open up new areas. Only in the most fertile valleys did people settle permanently as farmers, and in these places a more complex civilization evolved. The most important of these sites was the Kathmandu Valley, where a trade center developed from which the Kiratis exported woolen blankets and carpets and treated animal skins.

Gautama Buddha, the founder of a religion called Buddhism, was born in about 563 B.C. at Lumbini near the Indian border. Visiting the Kathmandu Valley in the fifth century B.C., Gautama Buddha toured Hindu shrines and preached his own faith. He converted some Kiratis from Hinduism—the predominant religion in the region—to Buddhism.

Two centuries later, during the reign of the fourteenth Kirati king, a Buddhist emperor named Asoka traveled from northern India to Nepal. At Gautama Buddha's birthplace Asoka set up a pillar to commemorate his religion's founder. He also visited the Kathmandu Valley and built a stupa at each of the four corners of Patan.

Charumati, Asoka's daughter, married a local prince named Devapala, and together they founded the towns of Chabahil and Deopatan. Although Asoka extended Buddhism throughout the valley, he never gained power in the region. Kirati rule continued until at least the first century A.D.,

Courtesy of Patrick Mendis

Prince Siddhartha Gautama (later known as Gautama Buddha) was born in the mid-sixth century B.C. at this site in the western terai. Until the age of 29, Gautama never ventured from the palace grounds where he was raised. Upon leaving the palace he saw an old man, a crippled man, and a corpse. These sights convinced him to give up his lavish lifestyle and wander in search of a solution to human suffering.

Photo by Daniel H. Condit

Tibetan refugees living in Nepal perform a Buddhist ritual of walking clockwise around a stupa near Patan.

after which the valley came under the control of the Lichhavis.

Lichhavi Rule

The Lichhavis invaded the Kathmandu Valley from India and controlled the region for several centuries. Under the reign of the Lichhavis, Nepal entered a golden age of arts, and Indian influence during this period was strong. The Lichhavis replaced the tribal democracy of the valley with a monarchy and divided the society into Hindu castes, or social classes. Hinduism spread alongside Buddhism, leading to the fusion of the two religions.

Manadeva I, the best-known Lichhavi king, ruled during the second half of the fifth century A.D. When Manadeva ascended the throne as a young boy, the Thakuris—a people living in the eastern part of the realm—took advantage of his inexperience by rebelling in an attempt to gain independence. But Manadeva possessed superior military skills and was able to suppress the rebels. Encouraged by his success, Manadeva then marched westward with his army and defeated the Mallas.

The Thakuris

In A.D. 602 Amsuvarman began the first Thakuri dynasty (family of rulers), inheriting the throne from his father-in-law, the Lichhavi king Vasudeva. A devoted worshiper of the Hindu god Siva, Amsuvarman also promoted the teachings of Gautama Buddha.

During this period Tibetan monarchs became increasingly powerful. Under King Srong-brtsan-sgampo the region came to dominate large areas of central Asia, including parts of China and the Himalayas. Amsuvarman arranged for his daughter Bhrikuti to marry the Tibetan king, perhaps in recognition of Tibet's power over Nepal. Bhrikuti brought Buddhist arti-

Photo by Bernice K. Condit

facts with her. With the help of Srong-brtsan-sgampo's second wife (a Chinese princess), Bhrikuti converted the Tibetan king and much of his realm to Buddhism. Indian forms of writing and literature as well as Nepalese art and architecture entered Tibet from Nepal and had a lasting effect on the region.

Nepal also had frequent contact with China during the seventh and eighth centuries. In 646 the Chinese established the first embassy in the Kathmandu Valley, and the Nepalese pagoda style of architecture may have been introduced to China at this time. Chinese travelers to Nepal marveled at the legacy of Amsuvarman. In particular they admired and wrote about his palace, which was seven stories tall and which was covered with gems and

Evidence of both Buddhism and Hinduism can be found throughout Nepal. Ancient rocks *(above)* that Buddhists have carved with *mani,* or prayers, dot the trails of Nepal. Monkeys *(right)* climb around a Hindu shrine at Swayambhunath. Hanuman, the monkey god, is revered by Hindus because he helped Rama— an incarnation (earthly form) of the god Vishnu—to regain his wife from a demon.

Photo by David Tykol

21

For centuries the Nepalese have believed that Buddha watches over them at all times. The eyes of Buddha, seen here on a doorway, are painted on many buildings to symbolize his presence.

Courtesy of Edith Lurvey

pearls. Gold fountains shaped like dragons surrounded the building, and the king sat on a lion-shaped throne.

Good relations between China and Nepal improved Nepal's prestige in India as well, because Nepal served as a vital link between Indian and Chinese trade. Indians acknowledged Amsuvarman as a Kshatriya—that is, a Hindu from the warrior caste. As it had done with Tibet, Nepal furthered its connections with India through marriage.

The Rise of Tantrism

The religious tolerance of Lichhavi and Thakuri kings led to the development of a new spiritual practice called Tantrism. A blend of Buddhism, Hindu philosophy, and popular folk beliefs, Tantrism may have arisen in Nepal as early as the seventh century. The new religion expanded Hindu beliefs and practices and inspired a Buddhist trend called Vajrayana, or the Path of the Thunderbolt.

Opposed to the life of contemplation encouraged by Buddhists, Tantrists substituted concrete action and direct experience as a means to achieve divine bliss. The movement greatly influenced both the local peoples of Nepal and their art, which often depicted physical pleasures.

Gunakamadeva

For the next several centuries, internal conflict in the Kathmandu Valley and foreign invasions disrupted Nepal, leaving its historical record unclear. According to the vamsavalis, several natural disasters —such as earthquakes and epidemics—

Photo by Amandus Schneider

A sculpture of Garuda, a man-bird who serves as the vehicle or attendant of various gods, is frequently found kneeling in front of shrines. With the body of a man, Garuda has large wings that fold out from his shoulders.

plagued Nepal, which could also explain the lack of historical information for the period. Two more Thakuri dynasties probably followed the one that Amsuvarman founded. Despite turmoil, trade flourished and settlements grew along the commercial routes.

A ruler named Gunakamadeva is said to have founded Kantipur (present-day Kathmandu) in 723, although a small community probably already existed at the site. He also introduced three major religious festivals and oversaw the construction of the Kastmandap, or House of Wood, from which Kathmandu would later take its name. After the reign of Gunakamadeva, the people of the Kathmandu Valley re-organized themselves into the separate principalities of Bhadgaon, Patan, and Kantipur. Joint rule by two or more kings became a common practice of Thakuri leaders.

The Mallas

The name *Malla* first appears in Nepalese historical chronicles in the fifth century and gains more frequent mention toward the end of the Thakuri dynasties. Although a Malla group is well known in Indian history, the Nepalese Mallas are probably not connected to them and may have arisen as a subordinate branch of the Thakuris.

The Sun Dhoka, or Golden Gate, at Durbar Square in Bhadgaon was constructed in 1753 by the last Malla king. Made of copper that is plated with gold, the door frame exhibits many gods. Above the door is Garuda eating serpents, his traditional enemies. The multiheaded goddess Kali rides Garuda. A gold-plated roof crowned with lions and elephants covers the gate.

Photo by Daniel H. Condit

23

The five-tiered Nyatapola Temple in Bhadgaon is the tallest (98 feet) in the Kathmandu Valley. Malla king Bhupatindra had the temple built in the early eighteenth century and dedicated it to a Tantric deity. Pairs of giants, elephants, lions, griffins (part eagle, part lion), and goddesses flank the stairs leading up to the sanctuary. Each ascending pair is regarded as 10 times stronger than the pair below it, and the giants—said to be the wrestlers after whom the Malla kingdom was named—are considered to be 10 times stronger than humans.

Photo by Bernice K. Condit

According to a legend in the vamsavalis, King Arideva heard news of the birth of his son Abhaya while he was wrestling. Thus, he bestowed the title *malla,* meaning "wrestler," to the infant, thus beginning the Malla dynasty in about 1200. Despite the meaning of their name, Malla kings proved to be more peaceful than warlike.

The Malla kings held absolute power and claimed to be incarnations (earthly representations) of Vishnu, the Hindu god of preservation. Although the monarchs strictly followed Hindu religious practices, they were also extremely tolerant of Buddhism, which was widespread among the general population—especially in its Tantric form.

Malla rule reached its peak under Jayasthitimalla, who conquered Patan in 1372. Ten years later he established a new Malla dynasty, which remained intact for the next four centuries. Jayasthitimalla unified the Kathmandu Valley, which had been in a state of civil war. He also introduced legal codes and expanded the Hindu caste system begun by the Lichhavis to include the whole population. Occupation, family status, and other social considerations determined which of dozens of castes an individual belonged to.

The culture of the people living in the Kathmandu Valley—who had come to be known as the Newar—flourished during the Malla period. Representing an ethnic and cultural mixture of the original inhabitants of the valley with Himalayan peoples from the north and east and Indians from the south and west, the Newar combined elements of various traditions. Skilled Newari artists and craftspeople developed a distinctive style that survives in the architecture, wood carving, and sculpture of Nepal. Newari, the language of the Newar, became the language of the king's court.

The Late Malla Period

After Jayasthitimalla's reign, the Malla kingdom declined under inefficient rulers. Regional officials began to assume more independence, which further weakened central authority.

In 1428, however, Yaksamalla began a reign that lasted more than 50 years, bringing unity and stability to the region once again. A supporter of the arts,

Photo by Bernice K. Condit

With a long artistic tradition, the Newar are perhaps best noted for their wood carving. Intricate designs grace the windows, door frames, pillars, and moldings of buildings throughout the Kathmandu Valley—the home of the Newar. Humans, gods, animals, foliage, and geometric patterns appear in various forms. The style and subject matter of Newari carvings have remained unchanged for centuries.

Courtesy of United Nations

Hanuman Dhoka (left), the royal palace in Kathmandu, dates from Lichhavi times, but most of its construction took place during the Malla period. Taleju Temple (right), which was built by King Mahendra in about 1549, is located within the palace complex.

25

Yaksamalla oversaw the construction of pagodas and other buildings and funded both Hindu and Buddhist places of worship. He also expanded the kingdom to the Ganges River in the south, to the Tibetan border in the north, to the Kali Gandaki River in the west, and to the modern Indian state of Sikkim in the east.

Yaksamalla arranged for his kingdom to be divided among his children upon his death, which broke the unity he had established. Although the valley continued to flourish economically and artistically, the Malla dynasty crumbled under political rivalries after Yaksamalla's reign and was overcome in 1769.

During the thirteenth and fourteenth centuries the history of Nepal began to encompass more of the regions beyond the Kathmandu Valley. Hindu Rajput princes who fled India during this period to escape Muslim invaders sought refuge in Nepal's western regions. The Muslim armies had come to India from the Arabian Peninsula in southwestern Asia and began converting Hindus to Islam. (Islam is the religion of the Muslims and was founded by the Arab prophet Muhammad in the seventh century A.D.) Although Muslims also entered Nepal and raided the Kathmandu Valley, they did not remain in the isolated region.

The Rajput princes established their own small principalities, which included as many as 46 states, to the west of the Kathmandu Valley. Each of these Nepa-

Courtesy of Air-India Library

The Royal Palace in Patan was the residence of members of the Malla family. An example of Newari architecture, the structure features artistic wooden and bronze windows and a gold-plated tower. Stone lions guard the entrance, and Garuda *(far right)* watches over the palace.

Photo by David Tykol

The wood carving on the Pashupati Temple in the Kathmandu Valley depicts common people, elephants, lions, griffins, and gods. The structure was built toward the end of the fifteenth century and is one of the oldest in Nepal.

lese kingdoms operated independently and continually engaged in warfare with its neighbors. The kingdom of Gurkha in central Nepal eventually asserted supremacy under the Shah dynasty, from which the nation's present rulers descend.

Gurkha Expansion

Established in 1559 by Dravya Shah, the Shah dynasty gradually expanded Gurkha territory over the next two centuries. In the mid-eighteenth century, Prithvi Narayan Shah embarked on a large-scale conquest of Himalayan areas. Known as a fierce and resourceful warrior-king, Prithvi Narayan Shah overpowered the kingdoms surrounding Gurkha, including those in the Kathmandu Valley. Taking advantage of the political instability of the Malla rulers, Prithvi Narayan Shah had assumed control over the entire valley by 1769.

Gurkha, the region from which the Shah dynasty expanded its rule, lies in the hills of central Nepal about 40 miles west of the Kathmandu Valley.

Photo by David Tykol

27

Courtesy of Todd T. Lewis

Prithvi Narayan Shah brought unity to the peoples of present-day Nepal at a time when chaos reigned. By expanding his realm to the Kathmandu Valley and beyond, he laid the groundwork for the modern nation of Nepal.

Prithvi Narayan Shah moved his capital from Gurkha to Kathmandu and called his new realm the Kingdom of Nepal. Composed of peoples from Nepal's three geographic regions—the terai, the hills, and the Himalayas—the kingdom was the foundation for the modern nation of Nepal. The king restricted trade with the British in India to prevent British colonial interest in Nepal. He also executed many people who he thought might threaten his position and the unity of the nation.

The descendants of Prithvi Narayan Shah continued Gurkha expansion. By the end of the eighteenth century Nepal's territory extended along the Himalayas from southern Kashmir in northwestern India to Sikkim in northeastern India—roughly twice Nepal's present size.

Foreign Conflicts

In the late 1770s Nepal became embroiled in a conflict with Tibet when the Shah rulers tried to assume the same privileges in trade and economics that the Malla dynasty had held. At issue were the circulation of Nepalese coins in Tibet and the taxation of goods traveling between India and Tibet.

Nepalese troops invaded Tibet in 1788 and 1791. China—whose powerful Qing dynasty exercised formal control over Tibet—ordered Nepalese troops to leave the region. When they refused, China sent an army of about 70,000 troops to Tibet. The Chinese army soon conquered the Nepalese forces and entered Nepalese territory. Nepal agreed to return Tibetan territory and to make a payment to Beijing, the capital of China, every five years.

With no possibilities left for further expansion to the north, the Nepalese turned their attention to the south. Their efforts to extend Nepal's southern boundary, however, came at the same time that the British were moving northward in India. When the British East India Company extended India's border to the boundary of Nepal, the Nepalese angered the British by raiding Indian territory. The Shah leaders also refused to establish trade contracts and diplomatic relations with the British in India.

To settle the dispute, Great Britain proposed that a joint commission discuss how to divide the territories. When Nepal refused to participate, Britain declared war and sent troops to occupy the areas in question. Nepal resisted a settlement for two years—until British troops entered the Kathmandu Valley—but in 1816 Nepalese leaders met British demands in the Treaty of Segauli. The agreement greatly reduced Nepal's holdings in the south, west, and east and established diplomatic relations between Great Britain and Nepal.

Although Nepal lost this war, the British had been so impressed with the performance of Gurkha troops that they

Courtesy of National Army Museum, London

During the Indian Mutiny in 1858, Indians fought against British colonists for control of Delhi, the capital of India. Gurkha troops from Nepal aided the British, who defeated the Indian rebels.

recruited Gurkha soldiers into the British army. Gurkha troops fought for the British in 1858 during the Indian Mutiny, in which many Indians rebelled against the British presence in India. In recognition of the loyalty of Gurkha troops, the British restored much of Nepal's national territory, and the country assumed approximately its present shape and size.

The Ranas

During the early nineteenth century a series of weak Shah kings made the post of prime minister an increasingly powerful position. By the late 1830s competition for the position had become bloody, and assassinations occurred frequently.

In 1846 Jang Bahadur assumed the position of prime minister by killing many of his opponents in the Kot Massacre and by exiling those who he suspected were not completely loyal to him. He filled the government administration with members of his own family and made the prime ministership hereditary. He and other family members added the honorary title *rana* (royal) to their names and stripped the king of his power.

After assuming power, Jang Bahadur traveled to Britain and France to broaden his own experience, but he initiated a strict policy of isolation for everyone else in Nepal. Foreigners rarely gained admission into the country. Those who did visit were severely restricted from contact with the Nepalese. This arrangement prevented the

29

Courtesy of United Nations

Kathmandu's Singha Durbar, or Court of the Lions, was the official residence of the Ranas. Built in 1901, the palace was patterned after Versailles in France and contains several courtyards and as many as 1,500 rooms. The building now houses the prime minister's offices and the National Planning Commission.

local people from learning of conditions elsewhere that were better than their own.

From 1846 until 1951 the Ranas held complete control in Nepal. Although they preserved the nation's independence at a time when European powers colonized most Asian countries, the Ranas did very little for Nepal's development. The Ranas stored up wealth for themselves, and their lavish lifestyle contrasted sharply with the poverty of most Nepalese.

Opposition to Rana Rule

During the 1930s and 1940s opposition to Rana rule grew throughout Nepal. The founding in January 1947 of the Nepali National Congress party by Nepalese who had taken refuge in India represented the first organized step in an anti-Rana movement. When the Nepali Democratic Congress party formed in mid-1948, opposition to the Ranas gained momentum. Both

groups sought to overthrow the Rana regime, and they united their efforts in 1950 when they merged to form the Nepali Congress party. King Tribhuvan, the powerless Shah monarch, secretly supported the aims of the Nepali Congress.

The independence of India in 1947 also aided the Nepalese struggle for a more open society. The Ranas had enjoyed friendly relations with India under British rule. When the British turned the government over to the Indians, however, the Ranas faced a regime that pressured them to make democratic reforms.

In February 1950, during talks with Indian prime minister Jawaharlal Nehru, the Ranas agreed to establish a bicameral (two-house) legislative assembly. The Ranas, however, delayed other political reforms, and uprisings broke out in the fall of 1950. When King Tribhuvan, who had been accused of involvement in a plot to kill the Rana prime minister, fled to

India in early November, rebellion erupted throughout the country.

Although the Rana prime minister proclaimed Tribhuvan's three-year-old grandson king, the Indian government continued to recognize Tribhuvan as Nepal's reigning monarch. By December 1950 Nepalese government troops had joined the opposition, and many members of the Rana family encouraged the prime minister to meet India's terms. In January 1951 the prime minister agreed to introduce several democratic reforms and to restore King Tribhuvan to the throne. The return of the king signaled the end of the Rana political monopoly.

The Return of Shah Leadership

The early years of post-Rana rule were unstable. For eight years the government alternated between a succession of administrations appointed by the Shah king and direct rule by the monarch himself. Internal disagreements weakened political parties. Disillusioned when improvements did not immediately follow the overthrow of the Ranas, the people of Nepal turned to

The only national emblem in the world that is not rectangular in shape, Nepal's flag is composed of two triangles, which at one time were two separate pennants flown together. The combination of red and blue is common in Nepalese art. The sun and the moon are traditional Buddhist symbols and suggest the hope that Nepal may live as long as these two bodies.

Artwork by Laura Westlund

the king as their main hope for unity and strength.

In 1959 King Mahendra—who had become monarch in 1955 after the death of his father, Tribhuvan—enacted Nepal's first constitution. The document created a bicameral legislature with a publicly elected lower house. The Nepali Congress party won elections held in 1959, and its leader, B. P. Koirala, became prime minister.

Mahendra criticized the rivalry that developed among the political parties, and he accused the leaders of the Nepali Congress party of corruption. In 1960 he dissolved the elected government, claiming that Nepal needed a democratic political system closer to Nepalese traditions.

In place of the old constitution, Mahendra enacted a new charter in 1962 that established a nonparty panchayat (village council) system. Based on traditional Nepalese village government, the panchayat system left most of the power in the monarch's hands when it was expanded to the national level. Under this arrangement, Nepalese voters elected village councils, whose members then chose district councils. District councillors selected representatives to the Rashtriya Panchayat, or national assembly.

Mahendra pursued the nation's economic development. He encouraged tourism and oversaw the building of roads and hydroelectric power stations. Mahendra also initiated a land reform program and sought to make it illegal to discriminate against a person based on Hindu caste. His son Birendra succeeded him in 1972 and continued these programs.

Growing Discontent

Despite the efforts of the Shahs to improve economic and social conditions in Nepal, the standard of living for most Nepalese remained very low. Popular discontent increased as the people became aware of their poverty and lack of progress

Photo by UPI/Bettmann Newsphotos
Born in 1944, Birendra Bir Bickrum Shah Dev became king of Nepal in 1972. He has continued the national modernization that his father began in the 1960s.

compared to other countries. In 1979 public demonstrations erupted throughout the country, and violence broke out in Kathmandu.

In response, King Birendra announced that he would hold a nationwide vote to determine whether Nepalese citizens wanted to continue the panchayat system of government or to replace it with a multiparty approach. By a narrow margin of victory, the nation voted to retain the nonparty panchayat format, and Birendra agreed to make the government more democratic.

Amendments to the constitution gave the Nepalese people the right to choose members of the Rashtriya Panchayat and granted this legislative body more power than it had previously held. The king, however, reserved the right to appoint 20 percent of the legislature's members and retained his ultimate authority. In response, some Nepalese continue to press for a more democratic system. In 1987 the Nepali Congress party encouraged people to express their dissatisfaction with the panchayat system.

Government

The Kingdom of Nepal's constitution, which was instituted in 1962 and revised in 1980, specifies that the monarch must follow the Hindu religion and that the king is the sole source of authority in the country. He presides over the unicameral (one-house) Rashtriya Panchayat and appoints a council of ministers, headed by a prime minister, to advise him on policy decisions.

Although the Nepalese people directly elect members of the Rashtriya Panchayat, the rest of the panchayat system follows a pyramid shape. Lower panchayats send representatives to form the panchayat at the next level—a process that extends from local to district to zonal panchayats.

All Nepalese citizens over the age of 20 can participate in the system at the local level. In addition to zonal panchayats, each of the 14 zones has a commissioner appointed by the king. At the top of the panchayat ladder, the Rashtriya Panchayat has 140 members, 112 of whom are elected every five years. The king selects the remaining 28 members.

Although the panchayat system excludes political parties, the government has encouraged former political party members to participate in the system. Thus, although parties remain officially unrecognized in Nepal, they are able to express their views.

A supreme court, whose judges are appointed by the king, heads Nepal's judicial system. The country also has regional, district, and zonal courts. The king can reverse any of the courts' decisions.

Courtesy of United Nations

Nepal has supplied the British army with Gurkha troops since the mid-nineteenth century. The income from these soldiers contributes to the economy of Nepal.

Photo by David Tykol

Each region in Nepal has its own distinctive style of architecture, which is determined largely by the locally available materials. Here, villagers at Ghanpokhara in central Nepal gather outside their homes. Stones form the base of these structures, and boards are used for the rest of the walls. Thatched roofs are common in all but the coldest regions of Nepal.

3) The People

Over thousands of years, various peoples migrated to Nepal from the north, south, east, and west, contributing to the nation's rich ethnic mosaic. Most of Nepal's 17.8 million people are subsistence farmers who grow only enough food to feed their families. The altitude, climate, and topography of the areas in which the various Nepalese groups have settled have influenced the ways they live. In addition, ethnic origins and history have shaped lifestyles, customs, housing, and outlook on life.

Most of Nepal's people are crowded into the hills and the terai, which has put severe pressures on the land in these regions. Although 93 percent of the population lives in rural areas, as social mobility and a sense of national identity increase, more Nepalese may begin to move to urban centers. Slowly, the nation's people are developing an awareness of themselves as Nepalese citizens. This new identity is added to their regional, religious, and ethnic loyalties, which traditionally have been very strong.

The official language of the country is Nepali, which derives from northern India's Sanskrit and which is the primary tongue of over half of the people. Other Nepalese speak various Indian languages. In the

Kathmandu Valley, Newari is widely used. At least 36 languages and dialects exist in the country.

Anthropologists have devised various systems to distinguish the peoples of Nepal. The broadest system groups all Nepalese as either Indo-Nepalese, whose ancestors came from the south and west, or Tibeto-Nepalese, whose ancestors originated in the northern and eastern Himalayas. Both categories are very general and include several subgroups.

Indo-Nepalese

Representing a majority of Nepal's population, the Indo-Nepalese include the Pahari (Hindu hill people), the Newar, and the Indians of the terai. All three groups are predominantly Hindu and rank themselves according to the Hindu custom of castes. Although the caste system in India has served as the model for the Nepalese arrangement, in Nepal the structure is less strict. Furthermore, a legal code enacted in 1963 prohibits discrimination based on caste and permits intercaste marriages.

Castes form a ladder of religious purity and social prestige. The priestly Brahmans and the warrior Kshatriyas (also known as Chetris in Nepal) are at the top. Untouchables—so called because they engage in

Photo by Daniel H. Condit

Many Nepalese women wear a round dot of makeup called a *tika* on their foreheads. Traditionally, the tika is a sign of having been religiously blessed, and it is found on certain religious symbols and statues. The tika has also come to be considered a beauty spot.

occupations that are considered unclean—are at the bottom. Dozens of other castes fall between these categories.

Particular castes vary from one group and one region to the next. Brahmans may be priests, landlords, or peasant farmers. Kshatriyas include landlords, landowning

Courtesy of Agency for International Development

Houses in the terai are typically made of bamboo that is entwined and plastered with cow dung or mud. Most houses in the region have one story and are covered with thatched roofs.

35

Photo by Bernice K. Condit

A Brahman man performs puja, or worship, which in this case is an offering—such as flowers, rice, or cloth—made to a god.

farmers, and tenant cultivators. Untouchables perform tasks such as blacksmithing, carpentry, barbering, farm labor, and scavenging.

PAHARI

Having strong Indian ancestral ties, the Pahari reside in the hills of Nepal, where they have intermarried with some Tibeto-Nepalese groups. Although most Pahari belong to high castes, they are not necessarily wealthy. Indeed, most are farmers who own small plots of land. They grow rice, barley, wheat, and corn and raise a few animals.

NEWAR

Although the Newar speak a Tibeto-Burman language and have Tibetan ancestors, centuries of close contact with India have placed them in the Indo-Nepalese group. Nevertheless, the Newar have retained a very distinctive culture. Borrowing some elements of Indian life, they have developed their own literature, architectural styles, religion, and decorative art.

The Newar live primarily in the Kathmandu Valley, where they comprise about half of the population. Although some Newar are farmers, traditionally they are

Photo by David Tykol

The hill region of Nepal features two-story houses made with mud bricks and roofed with thatch or sometimes slate. Buildings in the rainy east have steeply sloped roofs to ease water run off, while homes such as these near Gurkha have moderately sloped roofs because the area is not as wet. Verandas and courtyards, which serve as sites for family and social gatherings, are commonly part of houses in the hills.

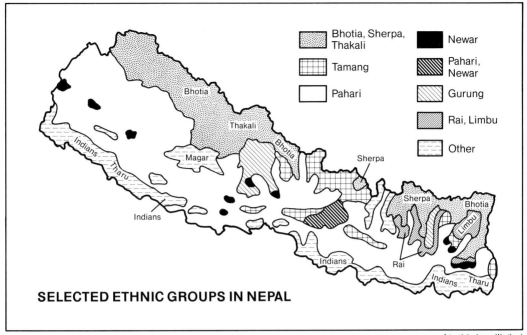

Bhotia, Sherpa, Thakali		Newar	
Tamang		Pahari, Newar	
Pahari		Gurung	
		Rai, Limbu	
		Other	

SELECTED ETHNIC GROUPS IN NEPAL

Artwork by Laura Westlund

Although each of Nepal's ethnic groups is concentrated in a specific area of Nepal, many are also scattered in small pockets throughout the country. Because of the mountainous terrain, many Nepalese live in isolated valleys.

traders and craftspeople. Because they are concentrated in the Kathmandu Valley, the Newar have played an important role in Nepal's civil and political life. They have a high level of education compared to other Nepalese, and, after the fall of the Ranas, the Newar began to enjoy economic prosperity. Since 1951 the king of Nepal has chosen his closest aides from the Newari population.

INDIANS

Although most of the Indians living in the terai are Nepalese citizens, culturally they are more related to the people of the Ganges Plain in northern India than they are to other Nepalese groups. The caste structure of these peoples follows that of bordering regions in India and differs from the caste system used in the rest of Nepal.

The largest of the ethnic groups in the terai is the Tharu, who also inhabit the neighboring Indian state of Uttar Pradesh. Once nomadic farmers, most Tharu now

live in permanent settlements and cultivate rice. Kinship unites Tharu villagers, who form tightly knit communities in which people work together. The Tharu worship Muslim saints as well as traditional Hindu and local gods.

Tibeto-Nepalese

The Tibeto-Nepalese represent a much smaller segment of Nepal's population than do the Indo-Nepalese. The Himalayas historically have cut people living in the mountains off from contact outside of their individual ethnic groups. This situation has prevented them from merging with other Himalayan populations.

Some Tibeto-Nepalese groups—such as the Tamang, Magar, Gurung, Sunwar, Rai, and Limbu—have lived in Nepal for centuries. A number of Bhotia (a name derived from the Tibetan word for Tibet), on the other hand, have arrived as recently as the 1950s, when they took refuge in

37

The vertical layout of Newari architecture has a distinctively urban flavor, although many Newar cultivate crops. Newari houses usually have at least three or four floors. The ground floor is used for storage of feed and fertilizer and for shelter of livestock. The second floor contains bedrooms; the third has an open space used as a visiting hall; and the top (usually the fourth) is a kitchen and dining area. Non-Newar houses, on the other hand, are usually only two stories, with a kitchen on the ground floor and with storage rooms and bedrooms above.

Photo by Amandus Schneider

Photo by Josh Kohnstamm

With Indian ancestral roots, the Tharu people inhabit the regions along Nepal's border with India. They are concentrated most heavily in the far western terai.

Photo by Josh Kohnstamm

Wearing a characteristic cap, a Tamang boy walks to school. Most Tamang live at high elevations in Nepal's north central hills.

Courtesy of Agency for International Development

The Gurung and Magar who live west of Pokhara typically build oval-shaped houses with thatched, cone-shaped roofs.

Nepal after the Chinese invaded their homeland.

Each ethnic group is concentrated in a particular area, but small numbers are usually scattered around other parts of the country as well. Most Tibeto-Nepalese earn just enough to live on through farming and raising livestock. Those inhabiting the mountains of the north lead a semi-nomadic existence, moving their herds from high pastures in the summer to lower elevations in the winter. Most Tibeto-Nepalese are Buddhists, but many have also adopted Hindu practices through their contact with Indo-Nepalese groups.

TAMANG

Living in villages in eastern and central Nepal, the Tamang subsist primarily as tenant farmers, load carriers, and wood-cutters. Villagers jointly own some land, and a *mulmi* (tax collector) collects taxes for privately owned property. A village priest, or *dhami*, performs seasonal agricultural rites and offers sacrifices to the gods. Large Tamang towns generally have Buddhist temples.

Photo by Josh Kohnstamm

Two Buddhist monks of Tibetan origin visit a stupa at Swayambhunath.

MAGAR AND GURUNG

Most Magar are farmers who live in the hills of central and western Nepal. Some Magar join the British Gurkha armies. Originally Tibetan Buddhists, many Magar have accepted some Hindu beliefs and practices after centuries of contact with the Indo-Nepalese. Many Magar communities have adopted Nepali as their first language.

The Gurung generally live higher in the mountains than do their Magar neighbors. They are shepherds as well as farmers, often depending mostly on their herds for a living. Like the Magar, the Gurung also become Gurkha soldiers, and some are successful businesspeople around Pokhara. Although many Gurung are Buddhists, those living at lower elevations in the southern portions of Gurung territory have adopted Hinduism as well.

RAI AND LIMBU

Considered to be among Nepal's original inhabitants, the Rai and Limbu peoples are thought to descend from the ancient Kiratis and are sometimes collectively referred to by this name. Both groups live

Photo by David Tykol

The Gurung people, who are noted for the striped blankets they weave, occupy some of Nepal's most inaccessible mountain villages.

Photo by Bernice K. Condit

A Tibetan saleswoman spreads out her wares in the Sherpa village of Namche Bazar. The word *bazar* indicates the the town is a market center.

in the eastern hills, with Limbu villages lying east of the Rai toward Nepal's border with the Indian state of Sikkim. The majority of Rai and Limbu practice subsistence farming, although some Rai join the Gurkha ranks. The Kiratis follow both Hinduism and Buddhism.

BHOTIA

The Bhotia, or northern border peoples, usually live at elevations of over 9,000 feet. Their culture, languages, and Buddhist religious practices are very similar to those of Tibetans. They farm in the high altitudes of the Himalayas, raise sheep and yaks, and participate in long-distance trade. Traders sell mountain herbs and spices, woolen scarves, leather goods, and jewelry.

Houses in the upper reaches of the Himalayas stand close together, often sharing walls with those next door to conserve heat. Most northern houses are two-story, stone structures, but some have mud walls. Roofs, which are usually made of slate or thick boards, are relatively flat so that they can hold an insulating layer of snow during the winter. In this village at Namche Bazar, a Buddhist monument surrounded by potato fields lies at the base of the hill.

Photo by Bernice K. Condit

Some merchants have gained wealth by smuggling expensive items—such as gold, electronics, and fancy clothing—from Hong Kong and Southeast Asia into Nepal. After the country was opened to foreign tourists in the 1950s, some Bhotia—most notably the Sherpa—have served as guides and porters (baggage carriers) on mountain-climbing expeditions.

Religion

Although Nepal is officially a Hindu kingdom whose monarch must be Hindu, religious practices in the country are very loose, and Hinduism and Buddhism exist side by side. Many Hindus have incorporated aspects of Buddhism into their faith, and Buddhists similarly have adopted elements of Hinduism. A third belief system, called shamanism, has also affected Nepalese religious practices. Shamanists

Photo by Bernice K. Condit

Holding a ritual bowl, into which believers put offerings, a Hindu holy man sits on a leopard skin in Pharping, south of Kathmandu.

Photo by David Tykol

At a temple in Kathmandu, the richly painted head of Buddha represents one of his many incarnations.

worship local gods, demons, and ancestral spirits, and they consult shamans (priests) to cure sickness and to control events.

Statistics indicate that about 85 to 90 percent of the Nepalese people are Hindus, and the remainder are predominantly Buddhists. The two religions are so intertwined, however, that this figure misrepresents the impact of Buddhism on Nepalese culture. Buddhist and Hindu temples are equally revered, and the Nepalese people celebrate the festivals of both religions. Consequently, many Nepalese regard the nation as being equally influenced by Hinduism and Buddhism.

HINDUISM

Unlike other major religions in the world, Hinduism has no single founder. The faith is based on four ancient texts called the Vedas, which were compiled in about 1200 B.C. Three main gods are central to Hinduism—Brahma, the creator; Vishnu, the preserver; and Siva, the destroyer. Individual Hindus choose their own form of worship. Hindu gods—especially Siva—are an in-

Photo by Daniel H. Condit

The Tantric god Bhairav—the fierce form of Siva—is said to reflect the appearance of humans when they are confronted with unknown forces. Usually painted black or dark blue, Bhairav holds weapons and human heads in some of his many hands. Often he is depicted trampling a corpse, a symbol of ignorance. The multiple limbs of Tantric gods represent the complete knowledge and all-presence of the divine.

Buddhists use mandalas (sacred diagrams) as an aid to meditation. These formalized, geometric designs have a specific arrangement of Buddhas, bodhisattvas (holy people who have almost reached the state of a Buddha), demons, and protectors. By visualizing certain circular images represented in the mandala and by chanting mantras (sacred sounds), meditators can orient themselves to the whole universe.

Photo by Josh Kohnstamm

tegral part of daily rituals in Nepal and symbolize the cycle of life.

Although the Hindu caste system is more flexible in Nepal than it is in India, castes play a major role in Indo-Nepalese life. A central belief of Hindus is that of reincarnation, or rebirth after death. Individuals who want to be reborn as a member of a higher caste must live a proper life in their present caste. Their actions (collectively called karma) in this and in past lives determine their caste in the next life.

BUDDHISM

Founded by Siddhartha Gautama in the sixth century B.C., Buddhism accepts or reinterprets many of the basic concepts of Hinduism. Gautama began teaching the new faith after he had renounced worldly life and had meditated for six years. This experience enabled him to attain enlightenment (the absence of desire and suffering), and he thereafter became known as Buddha, or "Enlightened One"—a title since given to Buddhists who are able to reach this state. Some sects of Buddhism

43

Photo by Bernice K. Condit

The Tengpoche Monastery is the leading center of Buddhism among Sherpa in the Everest region of northeastern Nepal. The imposing peak of Ama Dablam (22,493 feet) rises in the background.

encourage those who have reached enlightenment to refrain from entering nirvana (the highest level of enlightenment) in order to save others. These holy people are called bodhisattvas.

More a philosophy than a religion, Buddhism teaches that suffering is a result of attachment to people and things in a world where nothing is permanent. Mahayana, the Buddhist sect that took hold in Nepal, stresses concern for fellow human beings and universal salvation.

The Nepalese have also been strongly influenced by Tibetan Buddhism—an offshoot of Mahayana. Tibetan Buddhists believe that all things are interrelated. Thus, an individual person and universal cosmic forces are connected. Followers of the faith can tap this universal energy through meditation.

Another offshoot of Mahayana Buddhism, Vajrayana is practiced mainly by the Newar and borrows many ideas from Hindu philosophy. Vajrayana worships not only Buddhas and bodhisattvas but also five goddesses. This reverence for

female forces takes on elements of Tantrism, which seeks to attain nirvana in part through the union of male and female forces. Tantric practices influence all of Nepal's religions. Their popularity may be attributed to a philosophy that allows followers to reach nirvana in this life rather than after waiting through several lives, or reincarnations.

SHAMANISM

Perhaps the oldest religious practice in Nepal, shamanism involves the worship of pre-Buddhist mountain gods, spirits of diseases, ancestral spirits, and local Hindu gods. Shamanists entrust certain persons, called shamans, to communicate with supernatural beings. Most Nepalese—whether Hindu or Buddhist—incorporate some aspects of shamanism into their daily lives. Indeed, almost all of Nepal's ethnic groups have shamans.

While Hinduism and Buddhism focus on philosophical issues such as the nature of existence and the meaning of life, shamanism offers a way to deal with practical problems such as misfortune and sickness. The Nepalese believe that supernatural beings cause many illnesses and that only a shaman can determine which spirit has caused a particular problem. Shamans may prescribe herbal remedies as well as rituals to persuade a spirit to leave the patient's body. Sometimes, however, shamans allow local practitioners of folk medicine to cure health problems.

Health

Inadequate health facilities are among Nepal's greatest problems. As a result of rural poverty, many Nepalese suffer from hunger and live in substandard housing. Malnutrition and poor sanitation lead to many diseases and to early death. The

Photo by Bernice K. Condit

A family-planning billboard in Kathmandu describes the advantages of having only two children.

average Nepalese can expect to live to only 52 years of age. A high birthrate compounds the food shortages that many families face. In the hills and mountains, most farmers are only able to grow enough to feed their families for six or seven months of the year.

Although Nepal has an extensive river system, only 15 percent of the population has access to safe water because public supply systems have not yet been developed. Impure water supplies carry parasites that transmit intestinal infections. These ailments decrease the nutritional benefit that food provides and lower the population's resistance to disease. Partly as a result of poor sanitation, 112 babies died out of every 1,000 born in 1987. The figure is about average for southern Asia, but it contrasts sharply with the U.S. average of 10 deaths per 1,000.

Leprosy, tuberculosis, measles, and cholera threaten many Nepalese. The government, however, has successfully controlled malaria—which until the 1960s was rampant in the terai—and smallpox. The most pressing need for improved health among Nepalese is better sanitation—of food, of water, and of sewage disposal. In addition, the numbers of medical facilities and personnel must grow if they are to serve all of Nepal's people. In the 1980s Nepal had only one doctor for every 20,250 people and one hospital bed for every 5,000 people.

Photo by David Tykol

A Nepalese woman fills a jug with spring water. Few houses have running water, and access to an uncontaminated supply is a luxury enjoyed by only a small percentage of predominantly urban residents.

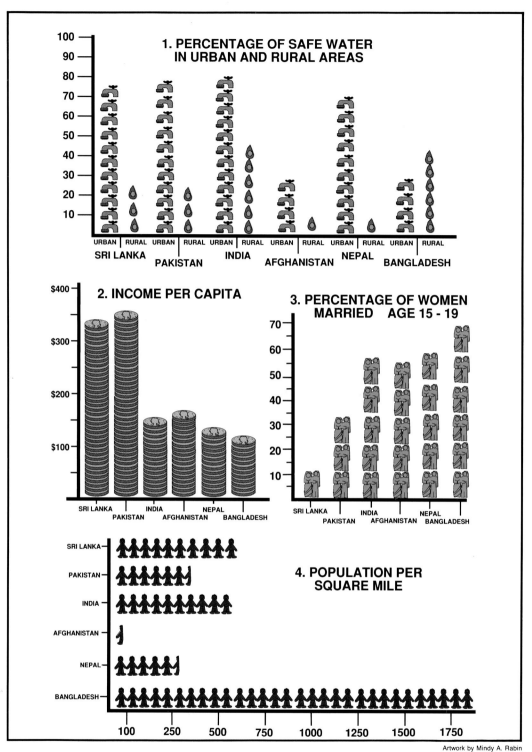

Depicted in this chart are factors relating to the standard of living in six countries in southern Asia. Information taken from "1987 World Population Data Sheet," "The World's Women: A Profile," and "Children of the World" compiled by the Population Reference Bureau, Washington, D.C.

Two girls bring home grasses they have collected as food for their herd of goats. Severe erosion has resulted from the Nepalese practice of cutting vegetation from the hillsides. Erosion washes away fertile topsoil, making crop yields lower and less nutritious. This situation has affected the diets, and therefore the health, of many Nepalese.

Courtesy of Patrick Mendis

Education

Although Nepal has inadequate educational facilities, the country's school system has made rapid progress since the 1950s. At that time only a few thousand children from the most privileged families were able to attend school. By the mid-1980s, 76 percent of Nepal's boys and 35 percent of the girls attended primary school, and 27 percent of the boys and 9 percent of the girls continued on to secondary classes. Literacy was up to 33 percent among males and 5 percent among females.

Gradually, as more villagers come to value the economic potential of education, more and more Nepalese are learning to read and write. A major drawback in the educational system has been a shortage of qualified teachers, but the government has made one of its main goals the improvement of the nation's literacy rate.

Primary schooling begins at 6 years of age and lasts for five years. Officially,

Photo by Bernice K. Condit

Schoolboys study together at a boarding school in Pokhara, located about 90 miles northwest of Kathmandu.

When weather permits, children at this school in Kathmandu have their lessons outdoors because classrooms are overcrowded. Nepal lacks enough educational facilities to accommodate all of its young people.

Courtesy of United Nations

elementary education is compulsory, but attendance is not enforced. Government-sponsored institutions provide free education. The secondary level begins at age 11 and lasts another five years. Only one university—Tribhuvan—exists in Nepal. It has several campuses in addition to the main one at Kathmandu.

Music

According to Hindu beliefs, music and dance originate directly from the gods. Legend says that the god Brahma sang the Vedas (Hindu sacred scriptures), repeating them continuously. Rudra, the god of lightning, is associated with song and dance and played a primitive form of zither (a stringed instrument). With these musical roots, the Nepalese view music and dance as more than just entertainment. To sing, to dance, or to play an instrument is to worship the gods.

Nepalese music has developed its own ragas, or melodic patterns (modes) upon which a tune is based. Different ragas are meant to represent a specific mood, a particular deity, or a certain time of the day or year. The choice of a raga is only a starting point, after which numerous variations

Photo by David Tykol

A *gaine* (professional musician) plays a four-stringed instrument called a *saranghi.* Traditionally, gaines travel from village to village and from festival to festival teaching and entertaining audiences with their songs of love, legends, and religion.

48

are carried out on the same theme, which can have a hypnotic effect on the listener. *Raginis,* the female version of a raga, work on the same principle but express a different set of moods and beliefs.

Each raga or ragini has a specific religious or social function and is played only under the appropriate circumstances. Traditional Nepalese music and dances are performed during the nation's many festivals. The Nepalese use mostly wind and percussion instruments. Like many other countries, Nepal is also influenced by Western music, and popular Nepalese music blends ancient and new styles.

Food

Most Nepalese consume subsistence-level diets that are based heavily on grains. In the southern part of the country, rice is the staple food, while at higher altitudes maize (corn) and millet are more available. The Nepalese make millet—one of the oldest of the cultivated cereals—into a flat bread or eat it as porridge.

At much higher altitudes, potatoes are the staple food. In the Kathmandu Valley, rice, millet, and maize are the main foods. Also available are many varieties of seasonal vegetables—pumpkins, green peppers, onions, and cucumbers, for example—

Photo by Daniel H. Condit

Musicians march ahead of a bride and groom after a wedding in Bhadgaon.

and fruits, such as apples, apricots, and plums. The Nepalese diet also includes a wide range of beans and peas, often served in the form of dhal (lentil soup).

Poultry, fish, eggs, and meat—from goats, buffalo, and yaks—are consumed in small quantities and usually only during certain festivals. Hindus are forbidden to eat beef. The country's most popular beverage is *chiya*—tea brewed with milk,

Photo by Bernice K. Condit

In Kathmandu two children operate a streetside stall from which they sell hot food to passersby.

A woman cooks with a new, fuel-saving wood stove. Fifteen thousand such stoves are being installed throughout Nepal, and authorities estimate that the stoves will reduce the amount of wood used as fuel by over 16,000 tons each year.

Courtesy of F. McDougall/FAO

sugar, and sometimes spices. The tea is grown in eastern Nepal. The Nepalese also brew *chang*—a type of beer made from fermented barley, maize, rye, or millet.

Nepalese food is very spicy—curries, chili powder, and ginger season the otherwise simple dishes. Food choices are closely linked with the numerous holidays and festivals, when the Nepalese indulge in more expensive foods, such as sweets made with molasses, sesame seeds, and nuts.

Art and Literature

Nepal has a rich artistic heritage that draws from Indian, Tibetan, Hindu, and Buddhist traditions, as well as from local sources. Although artistic expression suffered strict censorship under Rana rule, it has experienced a revival since the Shah family returned to power.

During two periods in Nepal's past—the seventh century and the eleventh to fourteenth centuries—Nepalese culture reached an artistic peak. Peoples throughout southern and eastern Asia admired and imitated Nepalese sculpture, painting, and especially architecture.

In the late thirteenth century Newari artists and architects—the best-known of whom is Arniko—were invited to Tibet,

where they introduced the pagoda and other Newari styles. Eventually, Tibetan motifs likewise found their way into Nepalese art. Chinese and Tibetan symbols, such as dragons and phoenixes (legendary birds), began to appear among Newari symbols.

The Newar became such skilled artisans that they are almost entirely responsible for Nepalese contributions to world culture. Consequently, most of the famous religious structures in Nepal are located in

Photo by Amandus Schneider

Eggplants, tomatoes, and cabbages are among the offerings of fresh produce at an outdoor market.

Courtesy of Todd T. Lewis

A Tibetan rug displays a dragon design in a skillfully woven repetition of patterns.

the Kathmandu Valley, the home of the Newar people. In addition to architecture, the Newar excel in wood carving; in copper, bronze, and brass work; in metal sculpture; and in painting.

The earliest written literature in Nepal dates from the Lichhavi period and uses Sanskrit, the language of northern India. Authors historically have written for a very small elite class in Nepal, since few Nepalese—even in the late twentieth century—can read. Instead of reading, villagers listen to storytellers, who carry on an ancient tradition of oral literature that predates the written word in Nepal. One common theme in Himalayan legends is the yeti, or abominable snowman.

Contemporary Nepalese writers usually favor the Nepali and English languages over Sanskrit. Authors who use Sanskrit tend to imitate traditional styles, but others experiment with new forms. Nationalist themes characterize the work of many young writers. The government's efforts to promote education and to increase literacy has encouraged authors to create more literary works.

Courtesy of Todd T. Lewis

Famed wood-carvers, the Nepalese have a long artistic tradition that has changed little over the centuries.

51

Photo by Daniel H. Condit

Merchants and shoppers mingle at a rice market in Kathmandu. Rice is Nepal's principal crop.

4) The Economy

Nepal's high mountains and isolated valleys have inhibited the nation's economic development. To compound this handicap, the policies of the Ranas held the country back until 1951, when the Shah family returned to power. In the 1950s the nation set about developing schools, hospitals, roads, telecommunications, electric power, and industry—aided by funds from India, China, and the United States.

Although the government has begun to build a basis for economic growth, Nepal remains one of the least developed countries in the world. Its average annual income per person was only about $140 per year in the mid-1980s—a figure that ranked among the 12 lowest in the world. Economic development has barely kept pace with the growing number of Nepalese, and authorities expect the population to place even more pressure on the nation's available resources. Overcrowding in Nepal's hill and terai regions has already caused serious damage. As people and livestock strip trees and vegetation from these areas, soil erosion and monsoon flooding increase.

To tackle the nation's development problems, King Birendra has established the National Development Council. Council members, who represent various sections of the country, advise the National Planning Commission on development needs and priorities. As a result, the latest economic plans have paid more attention to the rural areas of Nepal, where most of the people are agricultural workers who live in poverty.

The government has attempted to institute land reform programs to ease the hardships of farmers who rent land. So far, however, their efforts have been unsuccessful, and a few large-scale landowners continue to reap the benefits of land tilled by peasants.

Agriculture

Although over 90 percent of the population is engaged in agriculture, only about 15 percent of the country can be cultivated. One-third of this fertile area lies in the hills and supports over half of the population. Most of the remaining two-thirds of farmable land is in the eastern and central terai.

Nepal's mountains compose a large segment of the country, but their rugged terrain can provide the few highland inhabitants with only a meager supply of food. The terai—with its level land, fertile soil, good transportation, humid climate, and possibilities for irrigation—offers the greatest agricultural potential in Nepal. The middle hills, in contrast, are overworked, and erosion has become a major problem in the region.

Almost all of the farming in Nepal is done on a small scale by families who use traditional hand tools. A few large farms in the terai employ mechanized equipment. Most Nepalese live in rural villages and survive by growing barely enough rice, corn, wheat, millet, and a few vegetables for the immediate household. In many areas, the land cannot support the growing

Courtesy of F. Botts/FAO

A farmer works his small plot of land with a traditional wooden plow pulled by a pair of water buffalo.

53

Gurung women bring home baskets of leaves and grasses they have gathered to feed their livestock. The stripping of vegetation, whose roots hold soil in place, has increased erosion of Nepal's nutrient-rich topsoil, thereby decreasing crop yields. Furthermore, dangerous landslides can occur during the rainy season, when downpours wash away whole fields and threaten lives and property.

Courtesy of F. Botts/FAO

Photo by David Tykol

Rice straw is stacked in bundles by the side of a home near Bhadgaon.

Near terraced fields, women grind seeds to extract the oil, which will be used in cooking.

Photo by Daniel H. Condit

Photo by David Tykol

A young woman passes a blooming field of millet, one of Nepal's grain crops.

population for more than six or seven months of the year. Young men commonly leave for long periods to work in India, enabling them to send back cash to support their families.

In addition to corn, wheat, and millet, highland farmers grow potatoes. Tea plantations and fruit orchards have been cultivated in some regions. Fruits include mangoes, bananas, peaches, oranges, apples, plums, and cherries. In the terai, large-scale farms grow sugarcane and jute (a fibrous plant used to make rope) for export. In favorable years, Nepal can also export rice and potatoes, but when harvests are poor the nation must import grains to feed its people. Farmers also raise goats, buffalo, yaks, and sheep either for their wool and milk or as work animals.

55

Forestry and Energy Resources

Although the Nepalese have traditionally relied on the nation's vast timber supplies for fuel, for livestock fodder, and for building materials, the supply of this valuable resource has become dangerously low. In addition to the loss of forests through woodcutting and overgrazing, Nepal's location on the steep slopes of the Himalayas compounds the problem. Erosion, aided by torrential monsoon rains each summer, quickly strips the hills of rich topsoil and reduces the fertility of Nepalese cropland. On hillsides that have been stripped of trees, the erosion process occurs even faster. Some members of Nepal's National Planning Commission have predicted that the hills will become semidesert if deforestation continues.

Rural Nepalese clear forests not only to feed their livestock and to create fields for farming but also to obtain firewood. The country relies on firewood for 87 percent

Photo by Josh Konnstamm

A community poster urges Nepalese to conserve fertile soil through careful agricultural planning. The top portion illustrates an ideal landscape, with neatly terraced slopes and irrigated fields. The bottom half documents the reality of erosion at work on a hillside.

Photo by Bernice K. Condit

The way these wood sellers carry their heavy loads distributes the weight evenly down their spines. With deforestation a major problem in Nepal, woodcutters frequently walk for miles to collect a full load.

of its energy needs, which consist mostly of cooking, heating, and lighting in private homes. Electricity and imported petroleum satisfy only a very small portion of the nation's fuel demands. Because the dependence on wood is so heavy, far more timber is cut each year than can be replaced by natural forest growth.

One of the most urgent needs in Nepal is for alternative sources of energy—both for private households and for industrial development. Although exploration teams are searching for oil in Nepal, sources of petroleum, natural gas, or coal have yet to be discovered. Solar energy could be tapped, but the cost of importing solar

Courtesy of F. Botts/FAO

Forest workers build a pine tree nursery in the Himalayan foothills. The seedlings will then be transplanted to replenish badly stripped forests. The roots of trees help hold soil in place when rain washes the hillsides.

Industry

Most of Nepal's manufacturing activity is based on the natural resources and agricultural products of the country. Concentrated in the Kathmandu Valley and in southeastern Nepal, industry contributed less than 5 percent of the gross domestic product (the total amount of goods and services produced in a country in a year) in the mid-1980s.

Jute plants, sawmills, and sugar refining facilities are located in Biratnagar. The most important industries include food processing, vegetable oil extraction, and

Courtesy of United Nations

Nepal's many rivers afford the country an excellent opportunity to create hydroelectric power. Eventually, Nepal hopes to produce enough electricity to sell to neighboring India.

cookers, irrigation pumps, water heaters, and other equipment is very high.

The most feasible and plentiful prospect for energy lies in Nepal's many rivers, but the country has only just begun to tap this huge resource. Nepal and India have jointly undertaken two irrigation and hydroelectric projects on the Kosi and Narayani rivers. Developers are investigating the Karnali River in western Nepal as another possible site for a hydropower plant.

India has provided capital (the initial investment of money) for a hydroelectric project at Devighat in central Nepal, and China has built a facility on the Kosi River. The World Bank, Kuwait, and Japan funded a 60-megawatt hydroelectric site at Kulekhani, which began operating in 1982. As of 1989, only about 1 percent of Nepal's potential hydroelectric power had been tapped.

Two men spin colorfully dyed yarn *(left)* in preparation for rug weaving. Handwoven rugs *(below)* are prized for their rich hues and durability.

Photo by Daniel H. Condit

the manufacturing of paper, brick, tile, and construction materials. Cottage industries —small businesses run by families who work in their homes—produce textiles, furniture, and soap. Tibetan refugees weave beautiful carpets, the sale of which contributes to the nation's income.

Industrial growth remains slow because start-up money, expertise, and energy supplies are scarce. In addition, poorly developed markets, an inadequate transportation network, and competition from inexpensive imported goods hamper development. Jute and clothing were among the first industries to emerge in Nepal. They arose in the 1940s, when high prices in India encouraged private Indian and Nepalese investors to open plants in the terai, where these products could be produced more cheaply. Later industrial developments have depended on foreign aid from India, China, the United States, and the Soviet Union.

Trade

Nepal conducts about 80 percent of its trade with India, where it exports its jute,

Photo by David Tykol

Traditional Nepalese clothing is fashioned from cotton fabric in bright colors and patterns. Many women commonly wear bracelets, beaded necklaces, and ear and nose rings. Jewelry is not only decorative but also a sign of a woman's wealth.

Photo by Josh Kohnstamm

grain, and fruit in exchange for India's manufactured goods. Tourism and the earnings from Gurkha soldiers employed by the British army are also important sources of foreign income. Nepal usually spends more on imports than it earns on exports.

Although Nepal traded freely with Tibet until 1950, commerce with this region almost ended after the Chinese occupied Tibet. The caravans that had traveled between the two countries for centuries nearly disappeared in the early 1950s, but by the mid-1980s they began to move across the border more frequently.

One of the most important caravan routes goes through the 19,000-foot-high Nangpa La Pass. Yak caravans take cloth and manufactured goods from India into Tibet and return with salt, wood, and livestock (mostly yaks). Nepal's exports to

Courtesy of United Nations

A caravan of yaks carrying salt from Tibet by way of Nangpa La Pass on Nepal's northern border rests at a campsite along the trail.

other countries besides India and Tibet consist of jute and handicrafts—mostly rugs woven by the Tibetan refugees living in Nepal.

Transportation

Nepal has the fewest roads for its area and population of any country in the world. As a result, walking is still a very common way to travel. The lack of good transportation facilities has hindered the nation's industrialization. Gradually, however, Nepal is using foreign aid to increase the number of its roads.

Porters and pack animals still carry much of the freight within Nepal. Some of the cargo reaching Kathmandu from the Indian border comes part of the way by

Photo by David Tykol

Walking and cycling are the most common means of transportation in Kathmandu and throughout Nepal.

Courtesy of United Nations

Passengers at the Gurkha airstrip in central Nepal wait to board a Royal Nepal Airlines plane.

At the airport in Chitwan National Park elephants transport passengers to accommodations within the park grounds. Visitors can take safaris to view the park and nearby game reserve.

Photo by David Tykol

a ropeway (an aerial cable used to transport freight) between Hetaura and Kathmandu. Paved roads connect Kathmandu to Birganj on the Indian border, to Lhasa in Tibet, and to Pokhara. An east-west highway services the terai, and the Siddhartha Highway links Pokhara to Bhairawa on the Indian border. During the rainy season, mudslides frequently wash out portions of roads.

Nepal has direct flights connecting Kathmandu with India, Pakistan, and Thailand. Royal Nepal Airlines links Kathmandu with many remote parts of the country, forming the only rapid transport between these areas. The landing fields, with the exception of Tribhuvan Airport in Kathmandu, are usually pastures that are cleared of animals shortly before the plane is due to land. Many of these landing strips are so short that they can only accommodate STOL (short takeoff and landing) planes. Domestic flights are operated informally, and takeoffs are subject to the weather, to plane availability, and to various other delays.

Tourism

Because Rana rulers followed a strict policy of isolation, Nepal could not begin to develop a tourist industry until the return of the Shah monarchy in 1951. Since then, tourism has expanded rapidly, and money spent by foreigners in Nepal has helped to improve the country's economic situation. Tourism brings in about $50 million annually and, along with hydroelectric power,

Photo by Bernice K. Condit

Sherpa—which means "people from the east"—commonly make a living as porters for mountain trekking expeditions. Transporting loads on foot is the only means of shipment in much of Nepal.

Rafting the white waters in Nepal is a growing sport for adventurous tourists.

Photo by David Tykol

Photo by David Tykol

Three boys sit on a Buddhist mani (prayer) rock in central Nepal. People come from all over the world to experience the nation's culture and to see its rugged beauty.

62

Photo by David Tykol

A merchant at a market square in Kathmandu displays a wide array of wood carving and jewelry for sale.

offers Nepal its greatest potential for economic growth.

The country's location amid the Himalaya Mountains and its great diversity of topography, climate, wildlife, and culture provide numerous attractions for tourists. Nepal is very popular among those who come to view wildlife, to trek, or to mountain climb. The highest peaks—including Mount Everest—challenge the skills of experienced climbers.

Although the network of paved roads is small, numerous trails crisscross the country, offering leisurely access to much of Nepal. Indeed, trekking is one of the best ways to see Nepal, and hikers can hire porters to carry their gear and Sherpa guides to lead the way and cook meals. Trekking agencies in Kathmandu provide all arrangements for treks that range from rustic to luxurious.

In the Chitwan Valley visitors can observe wildlife and greenery of the terai at the Royal Game Reserve and at Chitwan National Park. The area around Langtang Valley contains vegetation ranging from subtropical forests to alpine plant life. Mount Everest is famous for its spectacular scenery. At an elevation of 3,000 feet, the Pokhara Valley has breathtaking views of some of the most famous mountains in the world—Macchapuchhare, Dhaulagiri, and Annapurna.

Future Challenges

One of the world's least developed countries, Nepal faces several pressing challenges that are made more urgent by the nation's rapidly expanding population. The government's goals include improving transportation, education, and medical facilities and redistributing landownership. Tourism—the biggest source of foreign currency—has helped the country to earn money, but Nepal depends largely on international aid to fund improvement projects. Although greater use of hydroelectric power could play a vital role in the nation's development, tapping this energy source also requires outside funding.

Panchayat democracy has provided each Nepalese with the opportunity to participate in political, economic, and social affairs. Yet with few economic resources, the challenge of improving the standard of living for the nation's increasing population is very great, and some Nepalese believe the panchayat system is ineffective. Nevertheless, panchayat democracy has succeeded in unifying the Kingdom of Nepal while allowing its people to maintain their rich cultural diversity.

Index